Dreams + Nightmares

Dreams + Nightmares

Poets Northwest Anthology

2023

Northwest Houston, Texas

Dreams + Nightmares
Poets Northwest Anthology 2023

Anthology committee:

Holly Jahangiri	Chair
Eric Blanchard	
Stephen Schwei	

Table of Contents

Foreword

Poets Northwest is a group of poets in the Houston area, primarily in the northwest region. We meet monthly to learn from each other and outside experts and share our poems. We sponsor an annual set of contests for members and celebrate all of our fine work. Check out the biographies at the end of this collection to see how widely these poets have been published.

As a further way to celebrate our craft and talents, we publish a collection of poetry every few years. For this anthology, we chose the theme of "dreams and nightmares." In addition to the wild ride our brains take us on in our nightly reveries, some of these poems feature the aspirations and disasters of our waking life.

We hope you enjoy the varied perspectives and expressions by these twenty poets and invite you to join us via Zoom or in person on the third Saturday of each month. See poetsnw.com to find out how to become a member and to view the details of our meetings, regardless of where you live.

You could be a part of our next anthology!

Thank you for reading our work. Reviews and feedback are always appreciated.

—Stephen Schwei, President

Acknowledgements

"California Dreams" by Judy S. Bunch first appeared in *The Bayou Review*.

"Bites of Death," "Dreams Out of Reach," and "Sensations Lost" by Forrest Martino first appeared in his book, *Respectfully Submitted - The Art, Photos, and Poems of Forrest Martino*.

"Dream of Recompense" and "The Drawn Cat's Dream" by Terry Jude Miller first appeared in his book, *The Drawn Cat's Dream*.

"07.20.1969 Blessings" by Rose of Sharon first appeared in her book, *Offerings, A Book of Poetry*.

"How to Plant a Dream" by Lisa Toth Salinas first appeared on Mustard Seed Farm & Market's Facebook page (online).

"An American Vet Visits Vietnam" by Lisa Toth Salinas first appeared in *A Book of the Year 2019*, a publication of The Poetry Society of Texas.

"Dream" by Stephen Schwei first appeared in *The Chachalaca Review*.

"mono no aware" by Courtney O'Banion Smith first appeared in *Vamp Cat Magazine*.

"Cover Story" by Carol A. Taylor first appeared in *The Barefoot Muse: A Journal of Metrical Verse* (online).

"A Homecoming" by Carol A. Taylor first appeared in *14x14* (online).

Poets Northwest Board

Stephen Schwei	President
Holly Jahangiri	Vice President/Programs
Lynn Grice	Treasurer Historian Membership Newsletter
Eric Blanchard	Secretary Publicity Chair
[vacant position]	Fundraiser & Events Coordinator
Angelique Barber	Contest Judge
Karen Mastracchio	Webmaster

In Memoriam

Poets Northwest recognizes and honors the following members who have left us since the publication of our last anthology:

Betty Kersh (*Founding Member*)	July 2022
Annette Schwartz	November 2021
Nancy Toth	September 2020

The Roofer

Angelique Barber

Israel came after all hail broke loose,
an icy flurry of golf balls damaging our roof shingles.
The day after Father's Day, he arrived at sunrise,
the best time of day for his work,
before the blistering Texas heat took the day.
He showed up with a crew of men
wearing wide-brimmed straw hats,
while he donned a new *Super Dad* T-shirt.
Any man who supported twin sons
by spending fourteen-hour days hauling
bundles of gritty shingles up to a hellishly hot
rooftop had to be a *Super Dad*.

The next morning Israel arrived dog-tired,
but greeted me with a *"¡Buenos Dias!"*.
His day would be identical to the day before:
Show up at 6:30 a.m.,
toss a seventy-pound pack of shingles across one shoulder,
heave it up a tall ladder to a hot hazardous roof,
throw down the pack; haul another one.
He spent his days in one-hundred-degree heat—
hauling, sweating, climbing, sweating, scraping,
sweating, crawling, sweating, hammering, sweating—
harnessing himself to an eighteen-dollar-an-hour dream,
he worked tirelessly to give his sons a better life.

Still Morpheus

Angelique Barber

The morning was so fresh
the sun still slept.
Its dreamy eyes
had yet to open and offer
golden hues of brilliant light.

Overnight, I had slumbered with Morpheus,
the shape-shifting god of dreams.
Even though nightfall had come and gone,
Morpheus remained still, motionless.
What of his claims to subconscious revelry?

Even though night had passed,
my sleep was serene and placid;
he had not traipsed through the sea
of my subliminal mind. But rather,
I had experienced calm soothing sleep.

Theos had poured peace upon my weary mind,
and I awoke lucid and refreshed,
no misadventures of the mind,
only a clean slate of sober consciousness
unblemished, pure, inspired.

False Hope

Eric Blanchard

I had a dream about you,
and it was like eating leftovers
of the veal piccata you made
that spring eve in 2004
before you went vegan,

save for the few times a year
you crave fish
or when mussels are the special
at one of the Michelin-starred restaurants
to which you are drawn,

because, to you, life
is all about flavor, or should be,
and you want life to taste rich
and melt in your mouth
twenty-four seven.

That recollection has left me
peckish and standing in the rain
for eight hours straight
with false hope of getting a seat
at The French Laundry.

It's Not Me

Eric Blanchard

Waking from a dream, you roll away from me,
toward the wall. I can hear you mumbling something
about "cheating bastard." I know

it's not about me specifically,
but your therapist says that you carry
residual PTSD and trust issues

from your mother, your father,
and every past relationship you've had.
I know it's not me.

Still, you shrug me off, when I try to touch you.
You give me the silent treatment all day,
and I walk on eggshells.

Tonight, I sleep on the sofa in the den,
and, at almost midnight exactly, I stir to the sound
of you sobbing on the floor by my side.

You say you had a nightmare and you're scared.
I tell you that you're safe, and I hold you tightly.
You whisper, "I'm sorry. I'm sorry. I'm sorry."

Remembering the Dream

Eric Blanchard

I am sleeping tonight
on an over-stuffed mattress.
It is lumpy but soft.
I roll into the basin
my body has spent
nearly a decade perfecting.
It cradles me in the dark,
comfortable and familiar.
I am letting the wind
outside my window
rock me, as I slumber, my
snoring shaking the rafters.
I am letting the clamor
of my rapid eye movement
act as my exercise
for the week, and I am
warm for a moment.
I am letting the song
of my digital alarm clock
represent the end of time.
I am remembering the dream
I had almost forgotten.

California Dreams

Judy S. Bunch

"Come to the West Coast; we'll start anew.
It will be different, it'll be grand;
We'll all live happily . . ."
His midlife crisis resists work.
He shouts hurt words, raises a hand,
    demands isolation, asserts the unreasonable,
        withdraws from all.
    NO LOVE

One job. Ongoing need for rent and food.
Two preteens: one boy without a bed
    one girl, the focus of his ire, without escape.
That Christmas they each receive
    a pocket notebook of coupons full of little
    promises like ice cream and movies,
    redeemable throughout the year.
    NO MONEY

Her secretary salary cannot quell the barrage of bills
    Before bankruptcy.
She swallows her pride, asks for assistance.
    They deem her income too much.
She alone cleans the rented spacious house he chose
    overlooking the cold and foggy ocean
    with the scent of honeysuckle in the breeze.
She buffers his assaults against her cubs
    as best as she can.
She becomes empty.
Just one more day.
    SURVIVE

Fevered Dreams; Anima Me

George Fredric Campbell

In quarantine
With limited visitation
Shadows and voids in vaporous quakes
Crossing my mind and filling memories

Diagnosis undetermined
Attendants in sterile mask and gown take
Blood samples and tests for known viruses
Hopes and fears among the mysteries of medicine

Delirium administers to delight
In quiet solicitude, everything aches
Studying the room in steady rhythm
With the brain in darkened corners, shivering

Time stops to be studied
In life's mysterious interlocking stigmas
Similarities to death, prevalent darkness breaks
And the happiness of the soul as that moment enters

Puncturing the pompous
Timing of the immortal one's mistakes
Awake now find the exit from
The black whole of nothing inside

In a place, dark and desolate
Have mercy on anima me who wakes
With eyes closed in quiet supplication. I ask,
who, what, leads me from my involuntary madness

Dream Within a Dream

George Fredric Campbell

Waking from a dream I'm a little perplexed
having slept in after a blues bust on the night
leaving me wondering how I got here, this far
from where I usually am and should be right now.

I can tell I'm in a country home, aromas of
bacon, eggs, and biscuits permeate my senses.

Expectations are not as they seemed last evening
yawn-stretch then wander out into the living area,
she is busy with all the same aromas around her.

Looking out a window, I surmise as in back, I see
several saddled horses tethered to a rail fence.
I'm beginning to try figuring out how this could be.

Along the margins I think I have a good idea
where this is going, now if I can put together
what seems to be the beginning of a different day.

Cowboy country is quietly being plucked and twanged
through several speakers from more than one room,
and I'm still in my stocking feet, feeling like I could
shift into some gear on first scintilla of request.

I think I know how this should work if familiarity,
is of any consequence, then I will try to make this
errant nowhere place feel like this no place is a
real someplace—on notice.

Now fully awake,
I have transcribed my dream from last night.

WW II – About An Early Dream

George Fredric Campbell

I'm five, playing in the yard, large dogs
looking fearsome came by
way of our neighbors, one poked its head
through the open gate.
I did not move away, remembering how
Dad always said don't show
fear to people or animals they will know
you are afraid and bully you.

Weather was articulating rain, from looks
of the sky it would be on me
before noon, plenty of time to climb our trees.
I liked it up there,
among the leafed limbs, where I could see far
out and beyond our yard, past the pastures,
or dream into my future.

A convoy of army trucks came by
on the highway, turning
in front of our place, parking along the grader
ditch, where they pulled
out some boxes setting them up as tables
to eat dinner.

Seeing me up in the tall limbs
one of the soldiers came over,
leaning on the fence he struck up a conversation,
wanted to know if I was afraid.
I told him I was a good climber,
he said he had a boy
at home that was about my size, but
they didn't have any trees to climb.

The dogs had been taking this all in
with special consideration for
the food being passed out I guess they favored
standing by for
a handout that was more available
than what I might have offered.

The Visitation

Mark Fishbein

There you were, Luiz Bonfá, in my dream,
Sitting in our living room with a Cuban cigar
As I played your compositions on my guitar.
You filled a long pinky nail with cocaine
From a silver vial around your neck
Patiently waiting for me to finish my audition
With a faint smile on your pencil thin moustache.

My father introduced you to me, right where you sat,
Teaching me his beatnik ways. He raved about you,
For hours switching sides of the album,
Careful not to scratch, with glassy gin martini eyes,
Posing with one hand on his belly
While the other raised with an open palm,
Shifting his weight from one hip to the other
Mimicking the rhythm of samba.

You said, "let me see your instrument,"
Plucked a note or two, and then off you went,
Tapping your thumb by the sound hole like a drum
While your right fingers shifted strum to strum,
The left hand jumping frets in a frenzied syncopation...

Why, why do we wake up from these dreams?
Some are so real we are haunted for years.
As long as I hold breath I will remember that scene,
When you played for me, and me alone, on the couch.
If some night you might come again, I beg you,
Oh I beg you sir, come back to that living room
So you can meet my father, then young too;

We'll all drink gin and smoke menthol cigarettes
As you play "Manhā De Carnaval"
And I will laugh until I hug my father in tears
As if weeping could make the dream last forever.

dream in the golden years

Mark Fishbein

hitchhiking on a dead-end road
to a dead-end town
i'm still waiting for a ride
but traffic is scant
the few truckers carrying stacks
of coffin planks pass by
they are forbidden to pick up stragglers
although they need the company

tractors and donkey carts give a smile
as the electric cars fly by
so step by crooked step i carry my load
and see way yonder beyond the hills
the town incandescent on the horizon
as the day molts into twilight
another night spent on the roadside
playing my old guitar like an archetype hobo
sitting by a fire and reciting to the green rose

it hurts   but i'm not surprised
the highway exit sign posted warnings
and it has now been years   years
the only thing that keeps me afloat
walking on the hot concrete of despair
is the vague vision of my entry
when i reach that dead-end town
to know my purpose reborn
where people will be cheering
as i take out my guitar
singing ballads from the stormy times

Rest

Lynn Roberts Grice

Once sleep was a joy,
then the dreams came –
hard and rough.
Chased by the past,
threatened by the future,
I'd awaken more tired than before.
Dread came with bed:
one position, then another –
no comfort.
Nighttime minutes tick to morning,
creep to dawn.
One day there will be relief.
Focus on pure thoughts.
Exorcize the demons.
Pour them out in ink.
Vanquish them to hell's chasm.
Free the good from their chambers
where time and age have locked them.
Empty the slop bucket of negativity;
drink from the cistern of purity.
Sleep deep and good.
Leave dread of night and day.
Rejoice in moonlight.
Dance in the dawn.
Praise God for His blessings.
Get rest for my soul.

To Finally Walk

Lynn Roberts Grice

It's not new to wait
she's on the 31-year plan
several lives later
wiser and older
finally
it happens
completion
a long journey's end.

To finally walk across that stage
mortarboard and gown
diploma soon to be in hand
once a ticket to the stars
now just a piece of paper, perhaps
young faces mixed with old
who appreciates it more
and does it matter?

Lynn Roberts Grice

Ate anchovy and
venison pizza for lunch.
Nightmares all night long.

Slumber

Daniel Hunter

I went to bed,
when my child was one.
I awoke to find
she was six.

Am I dreaming?

I fell asleep
with a six year old
on my lap.
When I awakened,
she was twelve.

I must never sleep again.

But I took a nap
in the noon day sun,
while a twelve year old played.
I woke up to find her twenty.

I lay in bed,
afraid to sleep.
But it's too late,
she is gone.

A Good Father

Daniel Hunter

Was I a good father?
I don't remember.
It seems a long time ago.
You were so young;
now I'm old.
I must have fed you,
clothed you,
held you.
I must have loved you.
Years have made
shadows of those
memories.
Were they real?
Or just dreams that
comfort me on lonely nights.

Resurrection

Daniel Hunter

Memories haunt me.
I bury them
in the daylight hours.
At night, they arise
from their tombs,
fresh from the darkness,
ready to feast again.

Discordant Dreams

Holly Jahangiri

Discordant dreams, a purple labyrinth
I've traveled, night by night—a path well-worn
And fragrant, lined with flowering hyacinth,
Enlaced in water hemlock, strewn with scorn.

Dream-death, a preview of eternity,
Is easy. Slipping smooth like gentle sleep—
Enrobed in chocolate, dark anxiety
Disguised; imaginary monsters creep

Entranced, they lurk around the lucid edge
Subconscious precipice, translucent veil
Of rising mist and sunlight's shimmering pledge—
Triumphant, sure that Death will once more fail

(For now) to drown us in its brief embrace
Though nightmare's shadows cling and leave a trace.

Staging the Battle

Holly Jahangiri

Imagination is a stage, where acts
The world. Each plays against the shadow self
That tries on dreams and hopes for what it lacks
To chase away the thing perched on the shelf

That fearful thing that no one talks about:
The laurel crown, "success," demands success,
And chips away at confidence with doubt,
While certain failure leaves no room for less.

Within the deepest slumber, hope's secure;
In dreams, we dare to dream, to risk it all,
No hardship seems too hard to be endured.
But with the dawn, our aspirations fall.

The things we face with courage in the sun
Will see our battles over nightmares won.

No Nightmare Dares Rescind the Dream

Holly Jahangiri

"Which is the true nightmare, the horrific dream that you have in your sleep or the dissatisfied reality that awaits you when you awake?"

—Justin Alcala

Horrific dreams! Do nightmares dare rescind
Offers to the heart's deep rumbling timpani?
Rhapsodic insight—*no*. To racing thoughts, unconscious:
Rest. Free from worry, fear, and stress
Imagination plays. Each night's dilemma
Freed of fetters, set adrift,
Is rough and tumble-tossed, lost in a tsunami,
Callously flung against the rocky shoals—
Diminished. Dissipated. And if
Returned—as nightmare fuel—to sap the somnolent chi,
Each day's delight will energize
And animate the dreams we dreamed,
Making mountains from the motes of dust that flitter,
Slip solutions through the gate that logic can't escape,
Leaving monstrous anxieties to drown in the penumbra,
Ephemeral and weak, where nightmares cast their pall.
A light illuminates and clarifies the conscious foci
Destined to vanquish this suffocating death of night—
To win, with satisfied reality, the waking day.

Angels Dance

Maxine B. Kohanski

I hear a rustling sound
and soft, pure voices
singing a sweet melody
in perfect harmony.
I lift my head from my pillow
and in the doorway,
a light glow reveals
two silhouettes
wearing long white gowns,
flowers in their hair.
They dance with grace –
arms outstretched
in synchronized motion
choreographed perfectly.
I am serenaded to sleep
by a lullaby dream
I will never forget.

Petrified

Maxine B. Kohanski

He leans on the stone wall.
I see only his form –
his arm reaching out,
grabbing the young woman
who I realize is me.
I struggle for survival,
tortured by rough hands,
a wide ring around my throat
so thick, impossible to remove
and it is getting tighter and tighter.
Suddenly I am in a deep river
struggling to reach the shore
and repeating the words,
"If only I can find a kind person. . ."
I am choking, giving up.

Finally, I wake
but the nightmare is not over –
my CPAP hose is wrapped tightly
around my neck.
I free myself, jump out of bed
and sit in my chair for two hours.
I am petrified, trying to shake off
what had just happened –
thankful I am alive.

Dreams Out of Reach

Forrest Martino

I spied a stack of papers laying in the street
A travel magazine, tire torn, but contents still complete

Pages showing Paris, Rome, and Tokyo
Tourist destinations… of places I'll never know

Ads with couples smiling, eating on the beach
Hungry, I tossed the book aside, these places out of reach

Even the cost of the magazine, I could not begin to own
My own travel lay ahead, 'neath the bridge I call my home

Sensations Lost

Forrest Martino

"tis better to have loved and lost,
than never to have loved at all"

— Alfred Lord Tennyson

A person, blind from birth, can't comprehend colors.
A person, deaf from birth, can't understand music.
One deficient of emotion, can't understand love's passion.

But a person born with sight, or able to hear sound,
or one who has experienced deep love...knows these exist.
When these sensations are taken away, loss is created.

When you are aware of what you are missing,
the heavenly dream of love becomes a nightmare.

As such, I painfully suggest to Mr. Tennyson...
that to have known deep love's passion,
and then to have it torn from your life,
is not better than to have never known it.
The salted dagger-gouged hole in your heart
is amplified by the knowledge of the love lost.

Bites of Death

Forrest Martino

Viper fangs impale the skin
and inject a spreading death.
Poison creeps through the veins,
until your dying breath.

The enslaving vampire bite
scripted in a movie scene,
is the same for all the people
on methamphetamine.

And like zombie stories, when bitten,
there is no going back.
Meth's a real-world horror film,
where your life will fade to black.

Smoke it, shoot it, snort it,
and now there's a pill form.
No matter how you're bitten,
dream lives become raging storm.

Dark fears of snake-fangs and zombies,
or the bloody vampire bite,
don't compare to the nightmare of meth...
that grips you day and night.

Deep Sleep

Karen Mastracchio

Nobody welcomes nightmares,
invites the dreams that slip sideways:

one, always alone, finds no way out
of dark passageways, mazelike,
anxiety saturating space;

crowds and busyness in which one
can find no person willing to explain the event,
feeling terror over purposelessness;

the vehicle ascending a curved highway,
careening off a ledge,
dropping into deep water.

Waking with a start, heart palpitating,
eyes opening to a familiar room,
breath by breath calm returns.

A security of wakefulness crowds out the subconscious,
worms burrowing back into the depths of dark earth.

Dream Stew

Karen Mastracchio

In the cauldron of unconscious mind
a wondrous stew is brewed:

> two cups sleep
> the kind that's deep
>
> dice memories
> like jujubees
>
> add bright imaginings so clear
> and sprinkle in a bit of fear.

Stir with a toss, mix with a turn
to serve up the best of dream stew.

In Winter

Karen Mastracchio

drowsy dreams in grays and muted blues
hazy visions of ghost memories
bare branches and icy winds fuel an emptiness
warmed in candlelight and Christmas cheer
endings/beginnings topsy-turvied under quilts
wakings/sleepings indistinguishable
black bear hibernations in and out of dream
dreams of green   dreams of sunlight
dreams of waking from life's despondency

The Drawn Cat's Dream

Terry Jude Miller

there's a pencil drawing
of my boyhood home
on the wall above my writing desk

drawn by a hometown artist
who saw fit to place
a tiny cat sleeping beneath
the grandfather oak in the front yard

there's an expression
on the feline face
of complete abandon, of being lost
in a forgotten summer
when a prequel version of me
played with a younger brother,
now past the veil over a year

I wonder if the cat has dreamed
the boys into existence again,
ever sees the brothers fishing
in the nearby creek

engulfed in the casual conversation
of pre-teen boys, their greatest decision--
what flavor popsicle to select
when mother calls them home

they did not know death then
with its many hollowed darkness

but night never falls on the house
in the drawing

somewhere, perhaps on the other side
of the sleeping cat's tree,
my brother digs for night crawlers

Dream

Terry Jude Miller

"Why, thou hast put him in such a dream,
that when the image of it leaves him he must run mad."
—William Shakespeare

listless world of dream
just beyond the razor-wire
of this heart's breaking

raise the dead from sorrow's ashes
let us wander by the river
where skipped stones wrote
wrinkled tales upon rippled waters

time carves canyons
that separate life
into then and now

oh, if only this good dream would endure
my waking, it would bend the hands of time
to obey the spirit's wailing

fantasy fades, as all good things must
but give me just a tick or two
before reality coils again
separating my beloved and me

Dream of Recompense

Terry Jude Miller

in sleep eyes dance beneath lids
watch the illuminated self deliver
guilt to the subconscious in fugue movements
short sad melody weaved
into vain pollen that covets everything
in yellow-green recall

downhill you take flight
above barbed fences
baseball diamonds beneath your wingless body
absent of players   silence rushes by
on the shoulders of a cloudless sky
as stars beyond the horizon
beg their turn at time

suddenly plummeting like a kite
that has lost its faithful wind
the earth circles and grows near
until you awaken
a pool of sweat lathers your back
and the scream no one hears
dissipates into the flowers
you forgot to dream

Nicole

Michael Owens

All my life I sleep at night undisturbed by dreams
Never floating quietly on the river among birds and fishes
Our children running among the wildflowers

That mix of surprise and pain
At 4 a.m. when you went to the bathroom
Then coming back to bed
Your toe slams into the leg of the bed
You shout grab your toe and fall to the ground
Hit your head and elbow at the same time
When I turned on the light
There was blood everywhere, you lay motionless

That was the feeling flooding back in me
when I answered the phone.

The hospital called with a simple request
for permission to harvest your organs.

We talked about it last year
When you came back home with the baby
After the surprise pregnancy
You did not tell me about.

Suddenly I was awake
Lying next to you.
Your snoring rattling the windows.
It must have been a dream.

Winner

Michael Owens

Sitting on a bent metal folding chair
at a chipped child's desk given like so many things
to this my tiny church.

Only God knows why I answered his call
to go and bring people to the Lord,
sometime I wonder if I may have misunderstood his voice.

Counting the collection plate from last Sunday
I find some church attendee has dropped
this envelope with a lottery ticket for next
Wednesday's Powerball drawing.

I expect they made some bargain with the Almighty
promising to quit drinking or stealing cars
as is the common practice of this tiny flock
of misfit humans I have tried to call to Christ.

With Wednesday night the numbers are drawn
at a time when I am fast asleep but with noon
I return to the white cinder block square I call an office
rummage around for the ticket and check the numbers.

That is when I wake up.
It is the never knowing that
gives me this torture-filled dream every night.

Dreams of You

Michael Owens

Ringworm like burrowing in one's skin dreams
of you arrive in the night unexpected and irritating
creating an unpleasant itch in my mind.

These dreams of you steal my sleep,
rob me of comfort, leave me exhausted much like
our past conversations how to load a dishwasher.

Somehow dreams foreshadow the horror you bring
like when the kids took an Uber and arrived unexpectedly
seeking refuge to hide from your rage, I had dreamed it.

Dreams are like hallucinations of your coming
dragging past conflicts in your bag of surprises
then I wake in a cold sweat, trembling in fear.

After my session this afternoon my online therapist
reminded me dreams are not real and I was never
married and you died three years ago, mother.

Dreaming of Reality

Jonathan Peckham

Each time I wake,
I have an unearthly feeling
Rules of gravity don't apply,
Horizon is often perpendicular
To what seems solid ground,
I am sometimes a rhinoceros,
Making me think for a moment
I am in someone's avant-garde play,
But I can actually see the horn
Directly in front of my eyes,
Which leads to a certain conclusion—
My transformation is complete.

Intermittently, of course, I have a dream,
A dream of life filled with predictability,
Pillbox houses all in a row
Have the same white picket fences,
Neighbors politely say hello,
I never get to know them,
I drive to and from what is called a job
Engaging in the most inane work
That seems to have little, if any, point
Other than to further the true work
Of destroying the very planet
On which life in this dream depends.

Finally, again, I awaken from the nightmare,
Returning to a reality far from stark,
And, suddenly, there by the turnstile
Stands my girl with kaleidoscope eyes,
Music rains from a diamond sky,
I am with a group of wildebeests
Eating chocolate steaks and eel stew,
Drinking mulberry wine with absinthe,
Trying to keep turtles
From crawling out of our soup,
Sitting at a table suspended in air
High above a flaming circus tent.

Inevitably, irregular night descends,
Pushing dimmer switches in my brain,
Causing dreamland to swallow me whole,
Plunging me fearfully into a nether world
In which responsibilities roam the Earth
Like great carnivorous dinosaurs
That chew you up for a midday snack,
Spitting out meager useless bones
That you can use in tiny droplets of time,
Doled out like candy on Halloween
To those who wear the right clothes,
Who go where they are told to go.

     JONATHAN PECKHAM

Outside of this dreamstate,
My life is a Salvador Dalí painting,
But slumber is a drab Grant Wood
That looks almost real,
If one doesn't look too closely
To see the artificiality of it,
The "just too perfect" landscape.
I walk, trying to make progress,
But feet stick in melting road tar,
While time rolls backwards over me
Like a giant paving steamroller
Trying to make me a living fossil.

Disguised as myself, I sleep,
Wishing I had that special power,
Power to wake up on command,
To bubble up to the surface
From the murky waters of this dreamscape,
To plunge headfirst into the light and air
Where every breath I draw has a life of its own,
Where art and creative demons
Live side by side in wonder,
Where the flowers grow like stained glass,
Where there is a beautiful bridge of mirrors
That will take you anywhere you want to go.

Sleep Came as a Liar

Jonathan Peckham

Sleep is a liar,
it comes disingenuously,
sidling up to you,
a perverted uncle,
groping you with its tongue,
a thief of time,
it distorts everything it touches,
it tries to control you.
Sleep is not to be trusted,
it has you call yourself names
that you don't recognize,
plunders your id and ego
for a pirate's treasure,
no more than 30 silver coins
that will vanish in thin air
once consciousness returns.
It will kill you every night,
stabbing at the very heart of you,
coming back for more,
you will wish you were dead,
revel in the deadness of night,
thinking you are gone,
but the lie of death is survived,
your unheralded life goes on.

Sleep lurks in day-shadows, waiting,
waiting for you to be weak,
looking for an opening
represented by drooping eyelids,
a small nod of the head,

a chance to force you to return
to capture your brain in a vice-like grip,
telling stories beyond your understanding.

The rusty gears of sleep
continue grinding machinations,
pulverizing a rotting corpse of thought
into a hamburger helper entree -
an unrecognizable stew,
neither appetizing nor nutritious,
a concoction of random experiences
and disjointed nonsense.

You vie for control, struggling to remember
that secret word you can say to bring yourself back
to the grey world outside slumber,
yet the word does not come, you must see the lies
and believe they are the truth—resistance is futile.

Fiberglass Canoe Nightmare

Rose of Sharon

Late day
Paddle trip on
Timber-infested creek,
Hull hole, portage, no one in sight––
Night falls . . .

07.20.1969 Blessings

Rose of Sharon

"Honor, greetings and blessings to you,
conquerors of the moon.
Pale lamp of our nights and our dreams."
          —from Pope Paul VI's Blessing to the Astronauts, July 1969

Honor, greetings and blessings to you,
high respect, great esteem.
Best wishes and goodwill,
divine favor, celestial dream

to you, conquerors of the moon.
Collins, Aldrin, Armstrong; Mike, Buzz, and Neil.
Space seekers, summit reachers.
Lunar landing, serenely surreal.

The moon, pale lamp of our nights:
Calendar inspiration, force of tidal sea,
lightly illuminate, faintly reflect
our eventide, then dark apogee.

Of our nights and our dreams:
Mankind's twilight, aspiration peers to blue.
And her peaceful presence glowingly concurs,
honor, greetings, and blessings to you.

An American Vet Visits Vietnam

Lisa Toth Salinas

"The soul can split the sky in two,
And let the face of God shine through.
But East and West will pinch the heart
That cannot keep them pushed apart..."
—from "Renascence" by Edna St. Vincent Millay

The soul can split the sky in two.
I see such dark, though Asian rays
rise brightly with the morning sun
and burn through warm, exotic days.
The heart can force the tears to run;
the soul can split the sky in two,

and let the face of God shine through.
Here, in this place of heartbreak – hell –
where men were tried and torn in two –
the sun shines still and temple bells,
ring cheerfully each afternoon
and let the face of God shine through.

But East and West will pinch the heart
though Heaven gazes on this place
and rivers run with life, and plants
grow places once burned desolate.
Now jungles heal. As vet, I can't.
But East and West still pinch the heart

that cannot keep them pushed apart.
This place will always burn with fire
of war within my memory.
Now tourist, I cannot forget
my time here as the enemy.
Not home, but close to heart. As vet
I cannot keep them pushed apart.

How to Plant a Dream

Lisa Toth Salinas

Start small
            Be ready to mustard-seed
your way through every expectation

Sometimes the growing of something good
takes more grit and dirt and desire
than you ever imagined

            Believe in the soil
and in your own fragile wings
Ready yourself to work them to exhaustion
            to fly
            to prove yourself unbreakable

This is hope   the patience to lay quietly
            beneath what we long for

To wait for the right moment
            to push a wing beaten path
            through an impossible sky

The American Dream Flickers on the Coal-Fed Stove

Lisa Toth Salinas

Hungry is the word to describe their longing.
They have taken leave so many times:
farewells to family, the sorrowing steps
from soil of motherland to uncertain deck
of a sea-going vessel. There they clung to hope
on a storm-tossed sea.

The too-soon burial of their first-born son
almost killed her. So close to being swallowed
by the infirmities of an immigrant city,
they have come here—near the source
of the Schuylkill River—to gasp for breath.
Its newly dug canals, a path to promise.
Its mountain air as fresh as an Irish wake
bemoaning a difficult past.

Ann and Patrick do not yet know Civil War,
striking miners starved to death, the hangings
of countrymen in the name of Molly Maguire.

They can only squint at the soft light of the future
as Ann makes a proud, handwritten note about
Patrick within the new Bible she has just acquired:
            "Became a citizen of the U.S. in 1825"

Ferry

Stephen Schwei

I race to the ferry
as the timer ticks down.
The clock shows 3 seconds,
then 1.2.
As it hits 0.0,
a gate descends,
spikes snag
all four of my tires.
Momentum propels me
forward,
I barely make it on.

My car makes
several trips without me
while I seek assistance.
My sister Joan helps out,
takes me back
to our childhood home.
I want to ask her,
broach the subject,
if she's been
vaccinated yet,
before time runs out.

I return to the ferry,
my car still mired.
She said no.
It will be dragged
off the boat
like a wounded animal,
heavy with the weight
of her decision.

Dream

Stephen Schwei

This morning,
I woke up paralyzed
unable to move
trying hard, but helpless.
Lying face down
I couldn't rise up
couldn't push up.
I questioned
should I be able to?
In my dream,
a large Black woman
was sprawled on top of me
holding me down
crushing me.
As hard as I would try
the weight held me down.

I got up.
The dream transitioned to reality.
The weight was gone.
I tested my extremities.
I could push up.

Had my subconscious mind
been sending me a signal
that carbon monoxide
was settling in,
hovering in the air?
Was I overreacting?

I shut off the a/c,
a highly unlikely source anyway.
I opened the apartment door
listening for a motor
that I had thought I heard earlier,
someone piping something lethal
to me and who knows who else.

All was calm, except me.
An hour later
I got back to sleep
letting fate take its course.

Slow Flash

Stephen Schwei

Wait!
No parachute?
Cue the events
of my life
to roll.

Stuck on the tracks
spinning my wheels
as a locomotive barrels,
the proverbial reel
ignites,
lasting
less than a second.

Yet this time, with no trigger,
night after night, my dreams
revisit segments and incidents,
re-releasing episodes in a prolonged story.

Jobs, roles, responsibilities,
mistakes, ineptitudes, happenstance
and serendipities. Mostly relationships.
Compressed and comprehensive,
slow-motion vignettes.

What happens when closing
credits appear? Is the review
complete?

Am I prepared
to accept what has befallen?

mono no aware

Courtney O'Banion Smith

Japanese term for the awareness of impermanence, a transient
wistfulness as well as a deeper, gentle sadness about this state
being the reality of life

After each betrayal, she bought herself
flowers, but only the ones on clearance—
bunches in clear cellophane rotting in buckets
hidden but discoverable
by those who knew where to look
in the grocery store's floral department.
Every time she imagined the other women,
she bought bunches of mums
shedding purple tear-shaped petals when jostled,
wilted roses, rainbow-hued buds too open and bruised,
or limp poms, heads downcast with all they'd seen.
Pretty soon, each room had its own bargain bouquet
pieced together with blooms on their way out—
just enough beauty left in them
to prove that, for a moment,
something beautiful had existed
even if her dream couldn't possibly last.

Future Memories on the Fourth of July

Courtney O'Banion Smith

Sometimes endings are when to start again
On nights of fiery skies and farthest shores.
The dogs whine before the fireworks begin–
Forgotten memories like lightless stars.
We remember how we forget again
That black and white flea market postcard bought
On a whim: Old naked couple, cold sun
Setting on white-capped waves, occasion caught
Silver and white like their hair. Curved, blurry,
Naked bodies sag just like us some day,
We'd say–our imagined longevity
Of a fake, endless moment, the way they
Face unknowable futures on the sand.
Skies explode. Dogs bark. We dream hand in hand.

Cover Story

Carol A. Taylor

My husband says I mumble in my sleep.
He says I sometimes sing, and often laugh.
He wonders what I've dreamed about. I keep
those little recollections to myself
and ask him what I said. He doesn't know.
He says it wasn't English anyway—
some language that he couldn't follow, though
it must be French or Spanish. I just say
I've no idea; I don't remember now—
maybe I was dreaming I was at work
or on the phone. Did I mention a name?
He says he doesn't think so. All the same
I plan to be prepared in case I do.
It won't be any problem to concoct
a likely explanation—*He's in the book
I'm reading*—if I ever mention you.
I'll shrug and stretch and yawn and say it seems
there's really no accounting for your dreams.

A Homecoming

Carol A. Taylor

I've hobbled down this road before.
I know these turns, the cul-de-sac,
the rutted, washboard lane, the shack
perched on a rock-strewn, battered shore.

It's not clear what I'm looking for,
though midnight promptings draw me back,
sleep-walker or insomniac,
to rattle at its boarded door.

And yet there's nothing lost to find;
no history worth returning to.
A single pebble in my shoe
confirms a path well left behind
when dawn illuminates the past
that wasn't good enough to last.

Dream of Dying

Carol A. Taylor

Do you ever dream that you're dying for air?
Trapped in a water-tight chamber somewhere,
you struggle to get out, holding your breath
in the dream, convinced that breathing is dying,
as though air were water or cyanide gas.
Then the ache in your chest overpowers resistance.
You gasp your surrender, endorsing your death,
though you know you're not ready. You let out your breath,
reinflate your sore lungs with a lethal concoction,
in equal proportion, relief and regret.

In the lull before waking, you know life is over.
The clock ticks, but death hasn't taken you yet.
Then hope resurrects as you surface in darkness,
inhaling slow drafts of relief and regret.

Writing Lessons

Jeff Ward

I meant to be a playwright.

Exparatastical Dreams, my "masterpiece" in teen naïveté,
was Beckett and Ionesco inspired: untold the transforming
of young George from dreamer to realist. I cherished the
depth encoded in every soliloquy, while my adoring fans
swore they read it. One friend's mom praised it, enraptured.
As Thespian president, I pressed the club to act out scenes,
and Mr. Lytle, our drama teacher, deemed it fine work. But
high school ends, transitions transform, our egos wane.

Weird college slug undone by broken relationships, pride
lost, confused about my roles in theater and the world,
wearing my desperation in long hair and bell-bottoms years
out of style, with spiritless aspirations, hope expired, I
burned four years rebuilding myself; yet still grasping
at the past, I recycled the play, rebirthed ingenious
characters, intensified the tension, hammered out my
doorway to a grand destination. *Now* it was great!

Turned in for my final project, a high mark certain.
Professor called me, said "What's this absurdist crap?"
Told me give him something he could read, so I spat
an ordinary one-act into existence that night. Got an A.
Never got my Exparatastical mistake back from him, but
no prob it was on my uncle's computer—until later that
summer when my cousin Mark wiped it with a factory reset.

Grief begat a clean break. This one moment, a key event
among several then, swiveled me to focus anew, more to life
than destination. In a way, my wonderful wife, my job, my
kids, and my dogs all emerged from that lost ambition.
But Mark, oh Mark, my unwarranted blame on you
faded too slow, seeing as how you helped shape this good
life, that I never let you forget until, to my regret I
apologized too late, in a quiet prayer at your interment.

Night Terrors

Jeff Ward

I am in bed, longing to be asleep.
I keep replaying a game from last evening.

I was contemplating my next move.
My phone rang. I moved my pawn. "Hello?"

I shuffle onto my side and try to relax.
It doesn't work. I roll onto my back.

Andy took my queen. Overwhelmed,
I almost missed Char's news.

I roll to a new side, and I blink at
the empty space beside me.

I should have protected my queen.
Char repeated: last night...Andy, with my...

The blankets are damp with sweat.
I hear my heartbeat in my pillow.

I said nothing but mindlessly took
Andy's rook because he took my queen.

I roll onto my stomach to muffle
a scream that wants to be free.

    Andy said I looked ill. He said,
      "Checkmate" and left to go home.

What could I have said? Could any
words get her back?

    I didn't stop him.
    I knew the game was over.

Montréal

Jeff Ward

I love Texas; I plan never to live
anywhere but here. Yet Canada looms
large in my dreams—perhaps another spring
visit to Montréal, in melting snow,
after work heading to a *cinq à sept*
to laugh and dine and drink with friends, and say
au revoir to someone I hardly know
(and quite likely will never meet again),
listening to a jazz quartet or to
the Québécois chat, half the words unknown.
Guy laughs and nods, teaching me the best of
the *sacres*. And I can't wait for morning's
outing to a snowy sugar shack for
a maple-covered breakfast in the woods.

About the Authors

Angelique Barber

Angelique Barber is an emerging creative writer and a twelve-year renal organ transplant survivor. She is a member of the Poetry Society of Texas and Poets Northwest of Houston. One of her greatest delights is spending time with family and friends. She lives in Houston, Texas with her husband, Ken. On sunny summer days, she can be found swimming like an otter and floating like a starfish.

Eric Blanchard

Eric Blanchard is a lawyer, an educator, and a daydreamer. He's a child of the past and a charter member of Generation X. His poems have been published in numerous collections, both online and in tangible form. In 2013, the online journal *Literary Orphans* nominated his prose poem, "The Meeting Ran Long," for Sundress Publications' *Best of the Net* anthology. Eric has published two chapbooks: *The Good Parts* (Finishing Line Press, January 2020) and *Beware of Poet* (Fort Worth Poetry Society Press, June 2022), which was the winner of the 2022 William D. Barney Memorial Chapbook Contest.

Judy S. Bunch

Judy S. Bunch became enchanted with poetry in her early teens when she went to a poetry meeting in Jackson, MS, at Eudora Welty's home, where Welty presided. She maintained that interest even though life has taken her in many different directions. She is not only a cat lady but is also a psychic happiest when being with others who have a passion for poetry and music.

George Fredric Campbell

George Fredric Campbell was born in rural Iowa, raised in Illinois near the Mississippi. Early schooling in one-room country schoolhouses. Has been a lifeguard, US Navy Hospital Corpsman, factory worker, schoolteacher, swimming coach, swimming school owner and National Parks volunteer. With wife Liz raised four children, welcomed eleven grandchildren, and twelve great grandchildren. Books include *The River Calls*, adventures on water; *WIWAK*, a memoir perspective of a boy, second-oldest in a family of seven; *The Mountains Call*, a world in the mountains he has made his own; and *Link – I Am Of The Earth*, nature's mysterious magic for all to see.

Mark Fishbein

https://www.poetwithguitar.com

A native New Yorker, Mark Fishbein graduated CCNY in 1971, and attended the Sorbonne in Paris for literature. He has five collections of poetry available, his latest being *Reflections in the Time of Trumpius Maximus*, (Atmosphere Press, 2021). He is Chancellor of PGN – Poetry Global Network's Poetry Academy, hosting workshops, classes, and Planet Poetry 28, a unique monthly online poetry journal, and is host to DC Poetry Workshop. A classical guitarist, he now lives in Chicago with his wife Elaine, where he is attending Columbia College for an MFA in Poetry.

Lynn Roberts Grice

Lynn Roberts Grice, married to David, has been a member of Poets Northwest since 2001, has served on the Board for 20 years, currently serving as Treasurer/Membership, Newsletter editor, and Historian. Poetry Society of Texas (PST) member since 2004, Councilor since 2008. She has won many awards for poetry, been published in numerous anthologies (including Poets Northwest, PST Summer Conference, Tyler Art of Peace, Waco Cultural Arts Fest, and *Blue & the Blues* by Pisces Publishing), four PST *Books of the Year*, the *Texas Poetry Calendar 2004*, and has two books, *Poiema*, 2007, and *Squirrel in a Cactus Garden*, 2011.

Daniel Hunter

Daniel Hunter has been a long-time member of Poets Northwest.

Holly Jahangiri

https://jahangiri.us/2020

Holly Jahangiri is the author of three children's books: *Trockle*; *A Puppy, Not a Guppy*; and *A New Leaf for Lyle*. She is one of the editors of the poetry anthology, *Walking the Earth: Life's Perspective in Poetry*. Holly draws inspiration from her family, from her own childhood adventures (some of which only happened in her overactive imagination), and from readers both young and young in spirit. She lives in Houston, Texas, with her husband, J.J., whose love and encouragement make writing books twice the fun.

Maxine B. Kohanski

Maxine Kohanski has been published as an award winner in numerous Poetry Society of Texas *Books of the Year*, NFSPS *Encore* and a wide array of poetry anthologies. A member of Poets Northwest since 1986, she has served on their board for many years and in many positions to include President. She was awarded The Hilton Ross Greer Service Award for her involvement with The Poetry Society of Texas. Previously self-published poetry books include:

Going Home, 1991, Heart Strings, 2010, *Shades of Gray, A Journey*, 2011 and *On Days Like This*, 2023.

Forrest Martino

Forrest Martino is a retired Engineer and longtime resident of NW Houston after growing up in Connecticut and Ohio. Forrest is new to poetry and thoroughly enjoys the Poets Northwest group. He volunteers performing music at Assisted Living Facilities. Forrest has a hunger to learn and seeks the simple pleasures in life. "The man is richest whose pleasures are the cheapest". He hopes to pass these values on to his five grandchildren living on Martha's Vineyard. <u>Dreams / Nightmares:</u> Forrest's dream is for a world with less hate and selfishness. His nightmare is the false information portrayed as news today.

Karen Mastracchio

By keeping journals and short writing assignments along with her high school students, Karen Mastracchio sowed the seeds from which her poetry emerged. After years of teaching the joy and craft of writing to others, Karen invested time in harvesting what had been dormant. She joined fellow poets at Poets Northwest and started sharing her poetry, submitting here and there. Karen's poetry has been published in several anthologies including *The Texas Poetry Calendar*, Poetry Society of Texas *Book of the Year*, and NFSPS *Encore Prize Poems*. Karen's chapbook *Seasoned* was released in 2022 by Finishing Line Press.

Terry Jude Miller

https://www.TerryJudeMiller.com

Terry Jude Miller is a Pushcart Prize-nominated poet from Houston. He received the 2018 Catherine Case Lubbe Manuscript Prize for his book, *The Drawn Cat's Dream*. His work has been published in the *Southern Poetry Anthology*, *The Lily Poetry Review*, *The Comstock Review*, and *The Oakland Review* and in scores of other publications. He serves as 1st Vice Chancellor for the National Federation of State Poetry Societies.

Michael Owens

Born in Galveston, Michael Owens is a botanist by training and writes from his home in Cypress Texas. Michael's work has been included in publications including: *Metonym Literary Journal* at Jessup University, *Red River Review, Houston Chronicle-After Harvey Poems, Poetica 2, The Inner Circle Writers Group*. His work has been in juried anthologies including *Texas Poetry Calendar, Houston Poetry Fest*, Poetry Society of Texas *Book of the Year, Austin International Poetry Society*. Michael has been a member of Poets Northwest for twelve years.

Jonathan Peckham

Jonathan Peckham was born in Troy NY and grew up in Syracuse. After getting his law degree in Washington D.C., he moved to Houston to start his commercial real estate law practice. He has been writing on and off all his life but has not made efforts to have his works published or otherwise recognized, so his poetry credentials are limited. He was a long-time member of Gulf Coast Poets before it dissolved, and prior to that and again currently a member of Poets Northwest where he recently won first place in the Bluebonnet Award in annual Spring Fling contests.

Rose of Sharon

https://www.RoseofSharon.net

Rose of Sharon is an author, educator, and poet. She loves daily encounters with the Creator and crafting words to honor those embraces. She hopes that while enjoying her writings, you will be inspired to pause a little and recognize the Creator's glorious Spirit in the world around you.

Lisa Toth Salinas

https://smallestleaf.com

Lisa Toth Salinas is a poet, genealogist, and author of *Smallest Leaf* (2015), awarded the Eakin Prize by the Poetry Society of Texas (PST). Her poems have appeared or are forthcoming in editions of the PST *Book of the Year* and NFSPS *Encore: Prize Poems*, and in *Presence Journal, St. Austin Review, Odes & Elegies: Eco-Poetry from the Texas Gulf Coast, Through Layered Limestone, Texas Poetry Calendar,* and *Keystone: Contemporary Poets on Pennsylvania*. Lisa is a two-time featured poet within the collaborative poetry & visual art exhibit *Color:Story*. She is honored to serve as Councilor-at-Large for PST.

Stephen Schwei

https://www.stephenschwei.com

Stephen Schwei is a Pushcart-nominated Houston poet with Wisconsin roots, published in *Wax Poetry & Art, Beneath the Rainbow, Hidden Constellation, The Borfski Press, RFD Magazine*, and *New Reader Magazine*. He has published one volume of poetry, *Bluebonnet Whispers*. A gay man with three grown children and four wonderful grandchildren, who worked in Information Technology most of his life, he can be a mass of contradictions. Poetry helps to sort all of this out.

Courtney O'Banion Smith

https://cobanionsmith.com

Courtney O'Banion Smith has a Master of Fine Arts in Creative Writing-Poetry from Texas State University-San Marcos, and she is currently pursuing a Master of Arts in

Theopoetics and Writing from Bethany Theological Seminary. A Pushcart Prize nominee, her work has appeared in various publications and anthologies including *Relief, Barren Magazine, Ocotillo Review*, and *Chaos Dive Reunion*. In 2022, the Poetry Society of Texas selected her book, *In Fidelity*, as the winner of the Catherine Case Lubbe Manuscript Contest. Find her on social media @cobanionsmith.

Carol A. Taylor

Carol A. Taylor is a retired translator and language teacher who lives near Houston. Her poetry has appeared in various journals and anthologies and is almost exclusively metrical. She enjoys rhyme and dialect. Carol served as Administrator of online workshop Eratosphere from 2001-2007 and Light Verse Editor of *Umbrella Journal's* Bumbershoot division from 2006-2008. She established the online metrical workshop Poet and Critic in 2007 and co-founded the bilingual reading group Alianza Poética Intercultural in Houston in 2012. Carol has four chapbooks, *Saving for the Future* (2003), *Houston Skyline* (2005), *Sonetos del Inglés* (2011), and *Telling It My Way* (2014).

Jeff Ward

Jeff Ward lives near Houston with his wife Cristina. Their children Arden and Evan recently moved out and into adulthood. In seventh grade, Jeff wrote a poem and liked it, which led to playwriting a year later. Inspired further, he started acting, felt destined to be a director, received a B.A. in Theatre from the University of Houston, and promptly started work as proofreader in a law firm. This led to being a director, accomplishing his early goal, albeit in legal information technology. Along the long journey, he has written a few poems. None have been published, until now.

Index of Authors

Thank you for reading our poems.

Please leave a review at Amazon, Goodreads, Barnes & Noble and other online retailers.

For more information about Poets Northwest, membership, and meetings, please visit poetsnw.com.